AAT

Elements of Costing

Pocket Notes

These Pocket Notes support study for the following AAT qualifications:
AAT Foundation Certificate in Accounting – Level 2
AAT Foundation Diploma in Accounting and Business – Level 2
AAT Foundation Certificate in Bookkeeping – Level 2
AAT Foundation Award in Accounting Software – Level 2
AAT Level 2 Award in Accounting Skills to Run Your Business
AAT Foundation Certificate in Accounting at SCQF Level 5

British library cataloguing-in-publication data

A catalogue record for this book is available from the British Library.

Published by:
Kaplan Publishing UK
Unit 2 The Business Centre
Molly Millars Lane
Wokingham
Berkshire
RG41 2QZ

ISBN 978-1-78740-300-0

© Kaplan Financial Limited, 2018

Printed and bound in Great Britain.

The text in this material and any others made available by any Kaplan Group company does not amount to advice on a particular matter and should not be taken as such. No reliance should be placed on the content as the basis for any investment or other decision or in connection with any advice given to third parties. Please consult your appropriate professional adviser as necessary. Kaplan Publishing Limited and all other Kaplan group companies expressly disclaim all liability to any person in respect of any losses or other claims, whether direct, indirect, incidental, consequential or otherwise arising in relation to the use of such materials.

CONTENTS

Preface

These Pocket Notes contain the key things that you need to know for the exam, presented in a unique visual way that makes revision easy and effective.

Written by experienced lecturers and authors, these Pocket Notes break down content into manageable chunks to maximise your concentration.

Quality and accuracy are of the utmost importance to us so if you spot an error in any of our products, please send an email to mykaplanreporting@kaplan.com with full details, or follow the link to the feedback form in MyKaplan.

Our Quality Co-ordinator will work with our technical team to verify the error and take action to ensure it is corrected in future editions.

A guide to the assessment

The assessment

The assessment will be in a single section.

Expect to see 15 independent tasks, several broken down into more than one requirement.

Learners will be assessed by computer based assessment (CBA) and will be required to demonstrate competence across the entire assessment.

The time allowed for this assessment is **90 minutes**.

Learning outcomes & weighting

1.	Understanding the cost recording system within an organisation	20%
2.	Use cost recording techniques	60%
3.	Provide information on actual and budgeted costs and income	20%
	Total	100%

Pass mark

The pass mark for the unit assessment is 70%

1

Cost classification

- Financial accounting and management accounting.
- The aims of management accounting.
- Cost accounting.
- Terminology – cost units and cost centres.
- Cost classification:
  - overview.
  - by function.
  - by element.
  - by relationship to cost units.
  - by behaviour.
- The Hi-Low Method.

Financial Accounting and Management Accounting

Characteristic	Financial Accounting	Management Accounting
Looks mainly at historical information.	✓	
Can include future forecasts and budgets.		✓
Formats dictated by accounting rules.	✓	
Content can include anything useful.		✓
Produced for shareholders and other external users.	✓	
Produced to help managers run the business.		✓
Produced in full once a year (and in some cases every 6 months).	✓	
Typically produced on a monthly basis.		✓

The aims of management accounting

Aims of management information

Cost accounting

Definition

Cost accounting is the process of calculating and recording the costs involved in the production and distribution of products and services.

Main reason for carrying out cost accounting: to calculate the cost of a product and therefore set the sales price of the item.

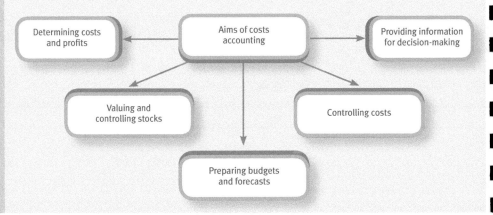

Determining costs and profits

Aims of costs accounting

Providing information for decision-making

Valuing and controlling stocks

Controlling costs

Preparing budgets and forecasts

Terminology – cost units and cost centres

Cost centre	=	area of business for which costs will be separately ascertained.
Profit centre	=	area of business for which costs and revenues are ascertained.
Investment centre	=	area of business where costs, revenues and net assets are ascertained.

Example

Cost centres

Manufacturing organisation

Production cost centres	Service cost centres
Assembly line	Stores
Finishing	Maintenance
Packaging	Quality control

Cost classification – overview

Purpose	Classification
Financial accounts	By function • cost of sales • distribution costs • admin expenses • finance costs.
Cost control	By element • materials • labour • overheads.
Cost accounts	By relationship to cost units • direct • indirect.
Budgeting, decision making	By behaviour • fixed • variable • semi-variable • stepped.

CBA focus

Make sure you understand the different types of cost classification as this is a very common exam requirement.

Cost classification – by function

Cost	Production = cost of sales	Distrib'n	Admin	Finance
Production labour	✓			
Production materials	✓			
Production supervisor salaries	✓			
Factory rent	✓			
Selling and distribution costs		✓		
Sales team commission		✓		
Delivery costs		✓		
Head office costs			✓	
IT support			✓	
HR support			✓	
Bank interest and charges				✓

Cost classification – by element

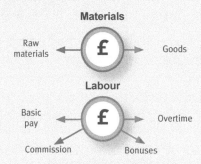

Materials

Raw materials ← £ → Goods

Labour

Basic pay ← £ → Overtime

Commission ↙ £ ↘ Bonuses

Overheads (expenses)

Cleaning costs ← £ → Power costs

Rent ↙ £ ↘ Rates

Advertising expenses

Cost classification – by relationship to cost units

- A **direct** cost is an item of cost that is traceable directly to a cost unit.

  For example, the cost of a bought-in lights for a car manufacturer.

  The total of all direct costs is known as the 'prime cost' per unit.

- An **indirect** cost is a cost that either cannot be identified with any one finished unit. Such costs are also often referred to as 'overheads'.

  For example, the rent on a factory.

Cost classification – by behaviour

A **variable cost** increases as the level of activity increases.

A **fixed cost** does not increase as the level of activity increases.

Graph of variable cost

Total cost £

Variable cost

Activity level

Graph of fixed cost

Total cost £

Fixed cost
(or period cost)

Activity level

Examples of variable costs:

Direct materials

Direct labour

Examples of fixed costs:

Business rates

Management salaries

A **semi-variable cost** is one that contains both fixed and variable elements.

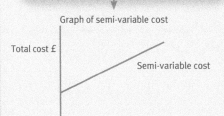

Graph of semi-variable cost

Total cost £

Semi-variable cost

Activity level

Semi-variable costs are also known as **semi-fixed costs** or **mixed costs**.

Examples of semi-variable costs:

Electricity costs – standing charge (fixed cost)
– cost per unit used (variable cost)

Salesman's salary – basic (fixed) + bonus (variable)

A **stepped cost** is one that remains fixed over a certain range of activity, but increases if activity increases beyond that level.

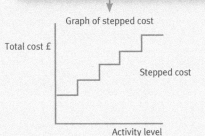

Graph of stepped cost

Total cost £

Stepped cost

Activity level

Examples of stepped costs:

Inventory storage costs

Supervisor salaries

The Hi-Low method

A method adopted to identify variable costs and fixed costs when only total costs are given.

The process:

Step 1: Consider all activity levels given, and identify highest and lowest (in terms of numbers of units)

Step 2: Calculate difference for these two levels in terms of numbers of units and total costs

Step 3: Calculate variable cost per unit: difference in total costs ÷ difference in total units

Step 4: Calculate fixed costs. This is done by taking either the high level of units or the lower (doesn't matter which) and working out total variable costs for that level – number of units x figure calculated in step 3. Then deduct total variable costs from total costs to find fixed costs.

Example

A company reports the following results for 3 months:

Month	Units	Total costs (£)
January	700	4,400
February	850	4,700
March	950	4,900

Step 1: Highest number of units is 950 in March, lowest is 700 in January

Step 2: Difference in total units is (950 – 700) = 250. Difference in total costs is (£4,900 - £4,400) = £500

Step 3: Variable cost per unit is £500 ÷ 250 units = £2/unit

Step 4: For 700 units, total variable costs = 700 x £2 = £1,400. Therefore fixed costs = £4,400 - £1,400 = £3,000

If we now want to work out total costs for an output of 1,100 units, it will be:

Variable costs (1,100 x £2)	£2,200
Fixed costs	£3,000
Total costs	**£5,200**

2

Coding of costs and income

- Classification and coding of costs.

Classification and coding of costs

Coding systems

- businesses make sales of various types/products and in different geographical regions
- they incur costs – materials, labour, expenses
- these costs need to be allocated to cost centres.

Coding of each sale and each cost incurred is a simple and efficient way of ensuring that the income and costs of the business are correctly analysed for management accounting purposes.

Desirable qualities of a coding system

Simple to understand

Comprehensive

In the assessment for Elements of Costing you will be required to carry out a variety of coding tasks. You will be given information which explains the coding system. Make sure that you read this carefully so that when you have to code documents or check coding done by others you fully understand how the particular coding system works.

Types of code

There are a number of different methods of coding data:

- numeric: e.g. 100/310
- alphabetic: e.g. AB/RT
- alpha-numeric: e.g. A230

Purpose of cost codes

The main purposes of cost codes are to:

- assist precise information
- facilitate electronic data processing
- facilitate a logical and systematic arrangement of costing records
- simplify comparison of totals of similar expenses
- incorporate check codes.

Example

Coding purchase invoices

A manufacturing organisation has the following coding system for costs:

Cost centre	Code
Machining	101
Finishing	102
Packing	103
Maintenance	104
Office	105

Classification	Code
Material	121
Labour	122
Expense	123

Specific	Code
Oil	131
Steel	132
Plastic	133

An invoice is received for steel used in the machining department.

Code   101 121 132

CBA focus

In the assessment you may be required not only to code a variety of sales invoices and purchases/expenses invoices received but you may also be required to check the coding that someone else has carried out.

3

Materials and inventory

- Different types of inventory.
- Valuing raw materials.
- Valuing WIP and finished goods.
- Calculating an overhead cost per unit.

Different types of inventory

Bought from suppliers

↓

Raw materials

↓

Issued to production cost centres who start making products

↓

Work in progress (WIP)

↓

Once items are finished they are usually transferred back into a warehouse

↓

Finished goods

↓

Finished goods then sold

Valuing raw materials

Need to value issues of inventory and closing inventory

	True	False
LIFO costs issues of inventory at the most recent purchase price.	✓	
FIFO costs issues of inventory at the oldest purchase price.	✓	
AVCO costs issues of inventory at an average purchase price.	✓	
LIFO values closing inventory at the oldest purchase price.	✓	
In times of increasing prices LIFO will give a lower profit figure than FIFO and AVCO.	✓	
FIFO values closing inventory at the most recent purchase price.	✓	
In times of increasing prices FIFO will give a higher profit figure than LIFO or AVCO.	✓	
AVCO values closing inventory at an average purchase price.	✓	

KAPLAN PUBLISHING

e.g **Example**

Swall Ltd has the following movements in a certain type of inventory into and out of it stores for the month of May:

Date	Receipts			Issues	
	Kg	Price / Kg	Cost	Kg	Cost
May 1	200	£4.50	£900		
May 2	100	£5.40	£540		
May 3				50	

Complete the table below for the issue and closing inventory values.

Method	Cost of issue	Closing inventory
FIFO		
LIFO		
AVCO		

Solution

Method	Cost of issue	Closing inventory
FIFO	£225	£1,215
LIFO	£270	£1,170
AVCO	£240	£1,200

Workings

FIFO

- The 50kg issued on the 3rd May will all come from the earliest purchase made on the 1st May.
- Thus the cost of the issue will be 50kg@£4.50 = £225
- Total purchases = £1,440, so closing inventory = 1,440 – 225 = £1,215

LIFO

- The 50kg issued on the 3rd May will all come from the most recent purchase made on the 2nd May.
- Thus the cost of the issue will be 50kg@£5.40 = £270
- Closing inventory = 1,440 – 270 = £1,170

AVCO

- We bought 300kg at a total cost of 900 + 540 = £1,440
- On average this works out at 1,440/300 = £4.80/kg
- Thus the cost of the issue will be 50kg@£4.80 = £240
- Closing inventory = 1,440 – 240 = £1,200

Valuing WIP and finished goods

Example cost card

The cost per unit for completed goods could show the following:

	Cost/unit £
Direct labour cost (2 hours @£10/hour)	20
Direct material cost	3
Direct expenses	1
Prime cost	24
Production overheads (2 hours @ £4/hour)	8
Total cost per unit	32

Direct costs

- Direct materials could be identified using job cards and information on stores requisitions.
- Direct labour can be identified using job cards and time sheets.

Indirect costs

- Unit basis – each unit gets the same level of overhead.
- Labour rate basis.

Calculating an overhead cost per unit

There are 3 approaches that you need to be familiar with for this assessment for calculating an overhead cost per unit. The 3 absorption bases are:

- A rate per machine hour
- A rate per labour hour
- A rate per unit

Example

Total factory activity for Johnstone Ltd is forecast as follows:

Machine hours	10,000
Labour hours	12,500
No. of units	60,000
Overheads	£150,000

Absorption rates can be calculated using the 3 bases as follows:

	Machine hour	Labour hour	Unit
Overheads (£)	150,000	150,000	150,000
Activity	10,000	12,500	60,000
Absorption rate	15.00	12.00	2.50

Factory cost of goods sold

	£
Opening inventory of raw materials	7,000
Purchases of raw materials	50,000
Closing inventory of raw materials	(10,000)
Direct materials used	47,000
Direct labour	97,000
Direct cost	**144,000**
Manufacturing overheads	53,000
Manufacturing cost	**197,000**
Opening inventory of work in progress	8,000
Closing inventory of work in progress	(10,000)
Cost of goods manufactured	**195,000**
Opening inventory of finished goods	30,000
Closing inventory of finished goods	(25,000)
Cost of goods sold	**200,000**

CBA focus

In the CBA you will be given a version of this with the rows mixed up. It is thus vital that you **learn the order**.

4

Labour costs

- Time related pay.
- Output related pay.
- Bonus schemes.

Time related pay

Output related pay

Bonus schemes

Payment method	Time-rate	Piece rate	Time-rate plus bonus
Labour is paid according to hours worked.	✓		
Labour is paid based on the production achieved.		✓	
Labour is paid extra if an agreed level of output is exceeded.			✓

Payment method	Time-rate	Piece rate	Time-rate plus bonus
Assured level of remuneration for employee.	✓		
Employee earns more if they work more efficiently than expected.		✓	
Assured level of remuneration and reward for working efficiently.			✓

5

Budgeting

- Budgeting.
- Variances.

Budgeting

What is budgeting?

Budgets set out the costs and revenues that are expected to be incurred or earned in future periods.

Most organisations prepare budgets for the business as a whole. The following budgets may also be prepared by organisations:

- Departmental budgets.
- Functional budgets (for sales, production, expenditure and so on).
- Income statements (in order to determine the expected future profits).
- Cash budgets (in order to determine future cash flows).

Budgetary control

The main reason for budgeting is to help managers control the business.

The budget gives a benchmark against which we can evaluate actual performance.

Any difference or variance can then be investigated to identify the cause. Once we know this we can take appropriate action.

Variances

| Variance | = | difference between actual figure and comparison figure. |

| Favourable variance | = | actual result better than comparison figure. |

| Adverse variance | = | actual results worse than comparison figure. |

Note: here the comparison figure will be the budget.

Example

Cost type	Budget £	Actual £	Variance £	Adv.	Fav.
Materials	24,500	26,200	1,700	✓	

CBA focus

In the CBA you need to be able to do the following.

1. Calculate variances.

2. See whether they are favourable or adverse.

3. Assess whether they are significant.

4. Assess who variances should be reported to.

Evaluating the significance of a variance

Management do not want to waste time investigating small variances, so will set criteria for deciding what makes a variance large enough to report and investigate.

For example,

- 'Only investigate variances bigger than £500'.
- 'Only investigate variances bigger that 5% of budget'.

If using a percentage measure then the amount of the variance that exceeds the cut-off percentage is known as the 'discrepancy'.

Reporting variances

It stands to reason that variances should be reported to the individual responsible for them happening, or who can take action on them.

For example, a Direct Materials cost variance that is due to materials price paid – report to Purchasing Manager.

Sales variance – report to Sales Manager.

Index